Stories

THE FAITH JOURNEY OF A HOUSEWIFE WHO HAPPENS TO BE NONVERBAL QUADRIPLEGIC

Laura Jean Pulscher

To Jean Rice
better known as Grandma

PREFACE

I can still see her matter-of-fact face, beautifully wrinkled with years of humble, loving service. "Write about what you know," Grandma offered as I rambled about my songwriting pastime.

Over the years, I have returned to that simple piece of advice frequently, ever finding it able to steer my creative efforts true. That guide has led me to value my own small experiences sufficiently to share snippets of my story with you.

In a technologically driven world, we have drifted from the quiet community found by gathering around a fire, enjoying the shared stories of our lives. Where is the oral storyteller? I strongly believe that the little stories of your and my lives hold power to influence the lives around us for the better as we taste each other's joys, foibles, and struggles.

My story is small. I am not the first person with ALS to share her story. But no one else has my story, and it holds significance.

May you benefit from hearing these stories, may you see value in your own stories, and may you serve those around you by sharing your simple stories too.

ON ACTION

Let there be space in this world for me

Let me act and cry in my shame

Or glory in a deed gone true or a word fitly spoken

Let the atoms of matter

And mankind's knifed judgment without mercy

   Withdraw and keep peace

Let me stand among the slings and arrows

To discover life's mysterious fortune:

The longing Fortune whispering

   Come, let us reason together

   Come, walk humbly with me

And as my time grows old

Let me learn to stand ready with bow and stone

   And listen

For the command that makes of my life

Such a grand intrusion upon this world

CHAPTER 1

Oh, the Beauty

Job 38:4–7 (ESV)
Where were you when I laid the foundation of the earth? Tell me, if you
have understanding. Who determined its measurements—surely you
know! Or who stretched the line upon it? On what were its bases sunk,
or who laid its cornerstone, when the morning stars sang together and
all the sons of God shouted for joy?

Sitting on a rooftop in Maine watching the Leonids streak across the sky, staring down at the glowing path our boat cut through the inky Gulf Stream waters of night, watching the rainbow hues of morning rim a star-filled sky from a small airplane window, watching a morning cloud spill over a mountain into a valley in the Australian Blue Mountains, the happy solitude of snorkeling fifteen to twenty feet deep, feeling the earth tremble beneath me with the approaching thunder of a storm, watching the silent passing of a lynx, watching little stems of blue light emanate from each finger as I took a nighttime walk on a frozen lake, watching the northern lights dance, swaths of daffodils coloring the landscape, watching a spotted eagle ray awkwardly burst out of the salt water into brief flight, swimming behind thundering falls, spring peepers in deafening and joyous song, swimming in bioluminescent glow, fireflies filling my imagination as I fall asleep, the triumphant gush of notes in Widor's

Toccata, my children's bright eyes ~ I have gloried in the beauty of the experience of life. This unrequested gift. This rich palette of the vibrant everyday. Life has its struggle and pain and weariness. But sprinkled throughout, there is treasure, there is wonder. My heart is full with these whispers of love.

THE ENCHANTED

*Written upon watching the somewhat comical
full-breach of a spotted eagle ray*

I was not made to fly

I am the sorcerer of the sea

A suspended alluring carpet

   Woven and charmed into life by the master weaver

No woman's arts can match my grace

The instant respect I command by subtlest movement

   No man has known

I am the gliding sorcerer

   And   I am bewitched by the glimmer of light's birth

       I am enchanted by the enveloping cool current's arising

       I am spellbound by the cradling expanse of my painted home

   And   I must –

Forgive my ungainliness, I was not made to fly

– I must

Rise above in sheer joy and praise

   Touch the unknown

      Glory

And in my own way clumsily return to my known

– I must, else my heart would burst

CHAPTER 2

The Genesis

Psalm 139:16–17 (ESV)
Your eyes saw my unformed substance; in your book were written,
every one of them, the days that were formed for me, when as yet there
was none of them. How precious to me are your thoughts, O God!
How vast is the sum of them!

When did I choose to be a Christian? Was it when I was three when I first expressed a desire to follow Jesus, but was left with no memory of the event? Or was it when I was five and decided that I wanted to devote my life to following Jesus? Or was it when I was a twenty-two-year-old and chose to believe what the Bible said about Jesus, even though I couldn't prove it and didn't fully understand it? I don't know. I have been in the process of becoming. I'm still becoming.

I remember my first conscious participation in ministry, being included with the adults in prayer before a worship dance, maybe four years old. I remember my first little Bible, King James with a picture of Jesus surrounded by children on its soft cover, now filled with the random colors, highlights, underlines, and notes of childhood. I remember sweet nights singing my heart and faith out an open window to the God both here and beyond. I understood the message of the book. A good, powerful God exists. I am like him, made in his image. I am not like him in his power and goodness. His justice requires that he treat me as I deserve for my poor choices. His mercy triumphed over his justice, and he himself took the painful results of my poor choices, fulfilling his justice, declaring me good, drawing me close, and making me even more like him. I felt the love. I was guided by his book. And thus passed the genesis of my faith.

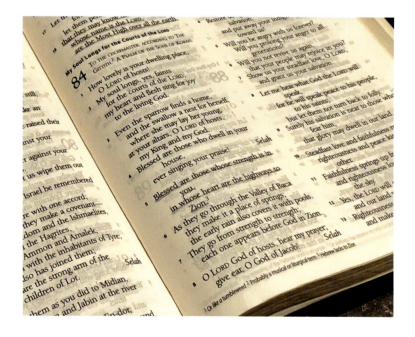

RESPONSE TO TIME

Love is my home
Peace is my cloak
I have seen that
Of which ancients spoke

At home I dwell
At rest inside
Precious, silent
Companion inside

CHAPTER 3

Messy Unity

John 17:20–21 (ESV)
I do not ask for these only, but also for those who will believe in me
through their word, that they may all be one, just as you, Father, are
in me, and I in you, that they also may be in us, so that the world may
believe that you have sent me.

Jesus prayed for the people who did and would love and follow him. One of his prayers was for unity: he knew that it would be a challenge to live together well. I have personally seen that challenge in a string of churches and Christian organizations. Depending on my proximity to the conflict, my experiences have ranged from disruptive to painful.

When I was under eight years old, our fun and joyous church, The Frederick Worship Center, became a center of conflict. I have beautiful memories there, from bobbing for apples and hay bale mazes, to singing Christian children's songs, to learning a Jewish style worship dance from the Messianic community, to exploring a discovery room made just for kids, to asking to be prayed over for prophetic anointing. The property had chestnut trees, I remember finding my first katydid there, and the old wooden building gave me a sense of mystery and awe. It was sad to leave the beautiful worship.

When I was maybe eleven, our family found conflict in our church, Fredericktown Baptist Church. I had the joy of performing in a musical there, even getting a speaking role. The church split. My father wanted to stay with the established church, my mother wanted to follow the offshoot.

I don't know how to begin describing the third conflict I experienced. This one hurt me deeply, and I was still processing the trauma at thirty years old. My beloved school, Frederick Christian Academy. The place where I made little, lifelong friends. Where I sucked sweet juice from honeysuckle, crumpled sassafras leaves for their heady smell, uprooted countless wild onions, found vines thick enough to make into a swing, and brushed past the inevitable poison ivy. Where I learned Bible verses and was encouraged to sing in harmony. Where I grew from a kindergartner to a teenager. At sixteen, I found myself in the middle of a school attempt at discipline. I was suspended, others placed on long term suspension and expelled. The experience did not seem to be guided by love.

The fourth and fifth final conflicts I was involved in didn't hurt me directly, but hurt me because they wounded people I love.

I had the deep joy to have the honor of working in the Wisconsin Northwoods with the team of wranglers at Honey Rock Camp/ HoneyRock for four summers and one full year. Back before the many acres had ever been logged and were speckled with silent giants. Back when there was ample evidence of its ramshackle, homespun, love-bathed origins, and where camp kids who grew up there dotted the landscape like shifting, elusive sprites – making sure the broomball ice was on point, training many of the horses, filling dorm rooms with canoes full of water, blending in with the forest, and literally putting out fires. We worked hard, we played hard, we sought God together. The camp was in a state of transition toward being more centered on serving college students. This was changing the camp from a loosely organized mission field to a more regimented extension of a college campus. And the backbone of long-term staff was being transitioned to individuals with higher education, housed off campus. The staff with less formal education and the camp kids were becoming a thing of the past, but they were also my daily present. My mentors, my coworkers, my boss. The changes came slowly. My heart watched my friends and mentors; I was there, but unable to help.

The most recent conflict I experienced was when I was twenty-nine. I don't know all the details of the conflict, but my beloved Central Baptist Church in Sioux Falls experienced conflict among the staff that led to larger-spread conflict. I did, however, know the details of the pain felt on both sides, and I loved deeply people on both sides of the conflict. Again, I was in a position where I could not help, so I loved and prayed and listened.

I am convinced that conflict will come to every group of believers. Whether the origin is sin, doctrinal differences, lack of love, or mission differences, living and working together will be messy. And sometimes we will be caught in the vortex and scarred. Jesus foresaw the pain, and prayed for us. We are his fallible church. He knows our weakness. He loves us.

PREACHER'S LAMENT

A few years, a few loves
Try to teach and to give direction
Stay close to the Lord
Thinking 'bout what's next and what am I to do
Sometimes I'm alone
Sometimes we worship as one
Hallelujah

A few tears and times are tough
Traveling in different directions
Stay close to the Lord
Thinking 'bout what's next and what am I to do
Sometimes I'm alone
Sometimes we worship as one
Hallelujah

God, hold the preachers' hearts
God hold the ones who serve
Give them peace
Give us grace
Give us all what we don't deserve
Be near when we're alone
Lord teach us to worship as one
Hallelujah

CHAPTER 4

Teaching a Hedonist to Trust

Isaiah 1:5 (ESV)
Why will you still be struck down? Why will you continue to rebel? The
whole head is sick, and the whole heart faint.

When I was twelve years old, God started working in my heart, teaching me to trust him. Up until that year, my life experience seemed nearly perfection: I had parents and a brother who loved me, I had good schooling, we lived in a good house with regular meals, and we were able to go on regular vacations. I loved my cat, Friendly, and I still enjoyed playing with Barbies.

It was when I was twelve that my Mom got lost in the woods overnight, then shortly after checked herself into a hospital for depression. When she returned home, my parents spent more and more time with voices raised in disagreement. It was while my brother and I were away from home visiting relatives that we learned over the phone that our parents were deciding to live separately. Thus began a new normal for us, living a week at a time with each parent.

How was my heart? Stunned and sad. Home was no longer a respite from the storm or a safe place in which to let my guard down. Home was no longer stable but a series of suitcases and backpacks. Home was no longer founded on the bedrock of devoted love. That foundation had given me a sense of anchored security, but in my new world, the line to that anchor had been cut, and I was adrift without knowing if it would be possible to reconnect to that security. Could I trust that the anchor of love in any marriage relationship would hold?

It is in the fear and unknown of being adrift that God revealed my heart toward him. I could have curled up in the home of the everlasting Love. I could have cried out my sorrow into the lonely nights and held my eyes up in trust that his love was ever secure.

I would love to say that I made wise choices, but I was a disillusioned hedonist, and I was faithful to my philosophy. I wanted to trust God's plan and love, but I felt that I should probably make sure that I was calling the shots in my life. If I worked hard enough and performed well according to my standards, maybe I could avoid the fracture of love that my parents had faced.

And year by year, my heart processed my parents' separation and my reaction, slowly understanding that I can't control my life. That God in his power can. That God is loving me in the middle of the mess. That his heart is good.

In the mess when I am pushed to the end of myself, my trust is exposed and given the chance to blossom. Even if it takes me more than twenty years to bud and bloom.

HOLD THESE DREAMS

Rough words through thin walls
I lay me down to sleep
There's another kind of death that kills
And that's not how love's supposed to be
All she wanted was to feel loved again
All he wanted was the great unknown
And a safe place to come home to

Take me out, talk me down
I trust so I tell you all
It was a quick way to clean up school
And that's not how love's supposed to be
All they wanted was less class disruption
All the kids needed was clear boundaries,
Fair warning, and to know somebody cared

Hold these dreams of mine
My life it's a little bit broken
Keep my young heart tender
Give me something to love

Here I am, sweet sixteen
Watching the loves walk out of my life
Looking for ways to pass the time and get away
All I wanted was to feel love again
All that you offered was all that you are to

Hold these dreams of mine
My life it's a little bit broken
Keep my young heart tender
I'll keep my eyes open
You give me something to love

CHAPTER 5

Like Heaven

Revelation 21:3 (ESV)
And I heard a loud voice from the throne saying, "Behold, the dwelling place of God is with man. He will dwell with them, and they will be his people, and God himself will be with them as their God."

The hills of the remote, Australian sheep station tossed and billowed like giant waves in shades of brown and green. After demonstrating on the ancient yet spry corral-escapee gelding Spartacus that I was not an imminent danger to my own welfare when riding, I had graduated. My novice thighs and rear hugged Rumba's saddle, carrying me like an awkward queen across dugout watering holes and hills. We checked on the sheep, and quiet Greg had his help collect one to be our evening meal. I didn't see him for a time while he was busy in a small, wooden building preparing the sheep. Around me wandered kittens and peacocks and incredible sheep dogs - working dogs attentive and obedient to the quiet instructions of their master. The sprawling house was simple but had what was necessary: running cold water, bedrooms, boots of various sizes. Dishes sat in a drying rack with the remnants of soapy water dripping off them, while with a twinkle in his eye, Greg told us tales of older days when it was impolite to speak of a lady's "limbs" and he had thought that women's feet were sewn on the bottom of their skirts. I only spent a week with Greg, but I treasure those memories among my fondest. To move with the rhythms of land and sky, to care for livestock, to feel the quiet, and all this permeated with the love of a time-taught man: nothing has ever spoken heaven to my heart like Greg Blaxland's Wellanbah sheep station of northern New South Wales, Australia.

I was in Australia when Greg passed away. His funeral was a train ride away, but the journey seemed unwise for a solo sixteen-year-old girl, so I was not permitted to go. A year later, my father and I visited Wellanbah. The land and horses remained, but the love ... the man who made it heaven was gone, and I could feel the difference.

Places can be painfully beautiful, but it is the beings, the lovers, in the places that make it heaven. When I change bodies from a solely physical to an immortal spiritual body, I will still find myself in places on the new earth. But as breathtaking as the landscape may be, it is only a setting for what will make it heaven: the presence of the Being of love. I look forward to seeing you there, Greg.

Attributed to Tecumseh:

"When it comes your time to die, be not like those whose hearts are filled with the fear of death, so that when their time comes they weep and pray for a little more time to live their lives over again in a different way. Sing your death song and die like a hero going home."

JUST LIKE HOME

I don't remember how it all began
The light the change the gentle hands
But slowly I woke up and I called this home
A mistake anyone could have made

And I slept under the stars
And I swam in a sea of lights
And I saw the sun rise above the soft curve of the earth

And I loved the power pulsating through the harness and the reins
And I loved the salt spray in my face
And I dared to call this home
A mistake anyone would make

I sat back and felt the sun on my face
While zeal and valor called my name
Courage steadied her aim
Victory crowned me her own
And I am forever changed

I am not home
Though I have thrown my head back and loved
I was born into a battle
And I wage my war through song
And when I find that I must die
This dust and these bones and my tired flesh
Will march home as a hero singing my victory song

And new blood will pulse through my veins
And I will finally see what He looks like
And it will all fit together just like home

And I will remember the battle
And what I had called home and what had made me homesick
And all my treasured loves
When my heart was not yet big enough
The beauty so raw it hurt
When I couldn't yet see half the whole
Mistakes everyone has made

CHAPTER 6

When I Am not Enough

Acts 17:26–27 (ESV)
And he made from one man every nation of mankind to live on all the
face of the earth, having determined allotted periods and the bound-
aries of their dwelling place, that they should seek God, and perhaps
feel their way toward him and find him. Yet he is actually not far from
each one of us ...

Sometimes, I am made painfully aware of my limitations. I don't know enough, and I don't have a wide enough frame of reference to properly process life events.

When I was sixteen, I was in eleventh grade at the small, Independent Baptist, King James Version-only school in which I had experienced the majority of my education. I was doing twelfth-grade history, math, and English, and I was looking into options for my senior year. Unfortunately, the school I had grown up in had no pathway for early graduation and was insisting I return the following year to complete one Bible credit. This arrangement did not appeal to me, so I began exploring other options.

When my father was about ten, his Australian mother brought his sisters and him to stay for a year in Australia while his developer father worked to build the family a home. The year at Barker College in the suburbs of Sydney had a profound effect on my father, giving him a hunger for learning he had not known before. Because of this transformative experience, he had offered to send my older brother to board at Barker in high school. My brother was not interested, but I remembered this option, and at this point it looked like quite an attractive option given the alternative of completing high school while attending the local community college.

My application to Barker College was quite late, and they had not had the opportunity to meet me in person, but somehow they agreed that having me join their school was a good idea.

So in January of 1996, I left my familiar but limited small class of twenty-odd kids that I had grown up with. I left my weekly migration between my parents' homes. I left a boyfriend. And I embarked on what would become a two-year experience of discovery. Those next few months would introduce me to a different culture where I bumbled around learning their rules, would gift me with the "freshman fifteen" weight gain a little early, forge strong friendships, inspire a love of academic learning, and shake my young faith.

My understanding of the Bible and my beliefs was reasonably solid for a sixteen year old. One of the strengths of exposure to an Independent Baptist environment was an emphasis on Bible memorization. I had grown up in a variety of traditions, including nondenominational charismatic, messianic Jewish, Baptist, and a smattering of Methodist, Brethren, and Episcopal. I had experienced two church splits, so I was aware of some challenges groups of believers could face. Both of my parents held their faith as a central part of their lives. I had even had the privilege of attending Summit Ministries summer camp, taking my brother's place when he decided not to go. That intensive course helped me better understand others' and my own worldviews, how they intersected and differed. And I had my own eleven-year journey of getting to know this elusive Being.

Finding myself in a new culture, my Independent Baptist background influenced me to want to reach out to the general culture and encourage them to seek God. So one Saturday I walked down to the local shopping area and handed out a few tracts – creative pamphlets about knowing God. While passing them out, I met Renee, a young woman who appeared to also love God. She offered to meet with me for Bible study before school at the nearby Maccas (yes, even McDonalds succumbs to the Aussie penchant for shortening names).

During our study, I noted a leaning toward perfectionism and unorthodox perspectives on baptism. Although I had already been baptized at age twelve, she believed I should be baptized again. I talked with my parents, and they agreed that I should not be rebaptized. So, although Renee and her church friends met with me at a pool with the intention of baptizing me, they agreed that I should obey my parents and not be baptized again at that time. Several friends from school had gone with me to the pool, and we walked back to the school.

Upon arriving back to the boarding school, our kind dorm mother expressed relief that I had returned and told me that because I had dealings with this religious group, the school might need to send me back to the United States.

I was stunned and hurt. I had been in Australia less than two months, and somehow I had offended my school possibly to the point of returning me home in dishonor.

The school and my parents asked me to have no further contact with Renee and her church. I obeyed and nothing more was said about the event by the school, other than having me chat with the Anglican chaplain a few times.

My father wrote to explain that the group had actually been a cult, sending pages of printed out information. I believed him, but I couldn't bring myself to read the papers because it hurt too much.

What I had not known was that another Barker student had recently joined the group, causing disruption in the school and leading to the severe reaction to my involvement.

The whole episode made me quite aware of my own limitations. Although I knew much of my faith, I could still exercise poor judgment on matters of doctrine.

Questions started gnawing at me. Could I trust the witness of my parents? What if they were wrong? How much had my culture influenced my beliefs? Was it possible to arrive at my faith through reason, devoid of revelation?

This event was the seed that eventually grew to maturity, leading me several years later to choose to completely renounce my faith and start from just my own limited experience of life to discover what beliefs made the most sense to me – suddenly becoming adrift in a sea of possibilities that included random meaninglessness. This journey was difficult, but I knew that I preferred to develop a robust system of belief and face whatever pain that entailed.

If the God of the Bible existed, he could handle my questions. And he would be faithful to reveal himself to one who seeks the truth.

WHY

Why would God want to talk to me
How could anything I say be of any need
To fill his cup
To lift him up
When he's bought out eternity

Why would God want to curb desire
Why need create a torture of fire
A just reward
They barred the Lord
Is all you really need a prayer

Why would God keep us in the dark
Why need keep us and knowledge apart
A mystery
That I believe
If I knew more where'd be my heart

Explain to me what I cannot grasp
All that I ask
Is that you help me to see

CHAPTER 7

Presuppositions, Meaning, Love, and Risk

1 John 4:16 (ESV)
So we have come to know and to believe the love that God has for us.
God is love, and whoever abides in love abides in God,
and God abides in him.

One of my kids sleepwalks. Several talk in their sleep. Not to be left out, I type in my sleep. I often wake in the middle of my sleep to find funny or nonsensical writings in front of me on my eye-controlled assistive computer. I have gone online in my sleep, texted in my sleep, and last night I deleted my first draft of this chapter in my sleep.

We do our best to make good decisions when we are conscious. Sometimes we make decisions in a semi-conscious state. Either way, personally I have found my mental abilities to be insufficient. Day after day I need to make decisions, and I don't know how to make the best decisions. Hindsight gives me a clearer view of the many ways I could have made better decisions. I'm not saying that to sound humble ~ I really am not wise enough to make good decisions. I chose a major I didn't understand or enjoy, I discovered that I am not a great leader by being a yearbook editor, I didn't even try out for my dream of being on a women's soccer team but instead joined the track and cross country teams (which I loved) then had to quit because I overextended myself. I don't understand why I make poor decisions. I don't know how to make better decisions. I still have to make decisions every day, from what I will allow my children to do, to what therapies will I try, to how much time will I spend entertaining myself versus seeking to contribute or learn. I try to make good decisions, but I am led by emotion, insufficient wisdom, and laziness even now. If I struggle so much to make these everyday decisions, what assurance do I have that I will make better decisions when it comes to the bedrock of my beliefs? I am limited and insufficient, yet I must still make these weighty decisions. I do my best, fully aware that my best and THE best are often quite different.

I found myself struggling in my faith after my experience with the Sydney Church of Christ. How did I know that my own beliefs were correct? Perhaps I had been unduly influenced by my parents. Perhaps I had not questioned my presuppositions and assumptions enough. Perhaps I had not given other belief systems serious enough consideration. In 1997, I applied to Wheaton College in Illinois as a Christian. I deferred enrollment, choosing to spend my first three semesters at less-expensive Baylor University. During my time at Baylor, I decided that the best way to come to beliefs with solid foundations would be to try to start from as blank a slate as possible. I became agnostic. I did not enjoy this decision, but I didn't know what would be a better option. My decision separated me from my Christian parents. My decision left me with no guide for morality. My decision took me from the warmth of a loving, present Being to the cold, empty expanse of uncertainty. Being an unaffiliated searcher was a lonely, unpleasant experience for me.

During this time, I decided to take as a presupposition that life has meaning. If I presupposed the opposite, I might as well end my meaningless existence. I decided that I would rather hope that life has meaning. As I thought about what gave life its meaning, I always came back to love, this precious intersection of vulnerable conscious beings seeking connection and the good of the other.

A necessary condition for love is the presence of conscious, sufficiently separate beings. It made sense to me that if love is central to existence, that there might be a Great Lover, a source of love. I chose to become a deist. I was attracted to the God of the Bible who claimed to be love. But I needed exposure to people who truly and deeply believed in that God to show me what that faith and love could look like in practice. People like that are not found everywhere, and it is not always easy to develop close relationships with them when they are found.

It was at this point that I transferred to Wheaton. I felt guilt being there ~ you are supposed to be Christian to attend. But I also really longed to see love and faith lived well. One of my previous friends had asserted that I would only find hypocrites there. That was a chance I was willing to take. I found the everyday, quiet acceptance of roommates. I found the simple faith of a small family that accepted me into their apartment for meals, babysitting, movies, and conversation. I found the opportunity to work with my hands loving horses in the northwoods of Wisconsin, guided by a man of quiet and simple faith. I chose the God of love of the Bible. I could believe in a Spirit too.

But Jesus.

Try as I might, I could not see why there was a need for Jesus to be an included person in God. I could not come to an understanding of that through my logic.

I knew that I could either spend my life uncommitted and unsure, or I could choose to accept what the Bible claimed about Jesus and risk being wrong. I decided that I would rather take the risk. Sometime around early 2002, I chose to become a hesitant Christian again. This time, I understood my presuppositions better: I chose to believe that life has meaning and that love is central to meaning. I understood why I chose the God of the Bible in particular. I understood that I was taking a risk including Jesus in my beliefs, and that I was willing to take that risk.

I doubtless could have made better choices on my bumpy road to faith. As evidenced above, I have ample room for growth. But this is the origin story of my faith. I stuck my flag in the sand and trusted the God of love to meet me there.

ORDER AND REVELATION –
DESTRUCTION AND CHAOS

I have walked the dark road
I have tasted the blackness
I have stumbled

I have stumbled on your steady hand
I have felt the lost Gilead balm pour across my weary mind
And I've struggled to make sense of it all
From my view here in the darkness

You beg me to search for and find the ancient paths
The generations of mothers and fathers before the pyramids and Ra
Before Gilgamesh, the well-worn path
You've hidden among the minutes and hours

I've got my best foot forward
My face held high
My hands at my sides
I follow the Way

CHAPTER 8

Learning to Live my Faith

Philippians 1:6 (ESV)
And I am sure of this, that he who began a good work in you will bring
it to completion at the day of Jesus Christ.

I am an imitator. I'm sensitive to the people around me, and I am likely to grow to resemble them.

As I chose to follow the God of the Bible, I wanted to know what it was like to participate in what the Bible refers to as the body of Christ, the church. My template for four summers and one full year became the fellow staff as I worked as a wrangler at Honey Rock Camp, now HoneyRock, run by Wheaton College in northern Wisconsin. Our focus was service and personal and spiritual growth, regardless of the activity: horseback rides, riding lessons, wrangler breakfast, wagon and sleigh rides, burro rides, mucking stalls, feeding the herd, playing broomball, and goofing off with the kids. We worked hard, we played hard. Sometimes we served well, sometimes we sought God well, sometimes we messed up. Slowly, with modeling of faithful people of all ages around me, and with practice, I grew.

There is no grand story to tell. Watching a tree grow is rarely an exciting affair, and my growth was little different.

HOLLOW

This was written over half a decade later,
but describes well the slow growth God was crafting

This is my history – a broken Christian family
Growing up a little fast, little leaves damaged in the frost
Oh I try to look high, but the truth is I am growing in the dirt
But by the grace of God I am what I am
Oh he's finding the hollows and filling them in

This is my here and now, a little growing family
I muster my strength, and life begins again
Oh I remember the frost and all that I lost
I think I see new growth again
By the grace of God I am what I am
He's finding the hollows and he's filling them in

I am so much closer to the dirt than to the sky
And my roots go deep and I can only reach so high
But I beg you please to fill the hollow spots
Where I lost leaves to what the locust and the frost have wrought
But I didn't see all you want to fill in me

Oh I was built to drink you in, I am hollow to the core
But by the Grace of God I am what I am
He's finding all the hollows and he's filling them in

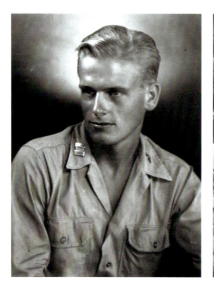

CHAPTER 9

To Ask for Help

Matthew 7:7 (ESV)
Ask, and it will be given to you; seek, and you will find;
knock, and it will be opened to you.

A young American GI approached the desk to get directions for his R&R time in Sydney, Australia. The needed information was given, but the GI remained unsatisfied. The pretty face giving the information inspired a new desire in the young man, and he asked whether she would like to accompany him dancing that evening. Honestly, she replied that she was previously engaged, and she suggested her friend for a date instead. The GI took her suggestion, yet vowed to never offer her such an invitation again.

He was not to keep his disappointed vow. Several days later, a friend encouraged him to ask again. She was not otherwise engaged, and, encouraged by her friend's glowing report of the GI's dancing, agreed to the date. She returned home to find that the GI had arrived early, and was having a chat with her father. The impertinence! Yet they continued to write postcards to each other as he moved to New Guinea, and as she joined the American Red Cross and was stationed in New Caledonia. On her birthday, she found a bouquet of flowers delivered, with regards from her GI. He had sent money with a pilot traveling to Sydney, who had passed it to another pilot traveling to New Caledonia. The GI was called back stateside in preparation for going to Japan. The young lady decided that she could create surprises too. Undaunted, with several friends, she boarded a troop ship headed for California, the only females among hundreds of soldiers. When she arrived in California, her GI was scheduled to immediately depart for Japan before she could surprise him. A superior officer got wind of the problem and delayed the departure. The surprise was a complete success! A week later, they were engaged. And that is how I got the privilege of an Australian grandmother.

My father has always had a deep love for his mother's homeland. Spurred by his love of both adventure and Australia, in 2006 he began a nearly three-year voyage from his home state of Maryland to Sydney, where his mother still lived with his stepfather. I had the great privilege of joining him from Maryland to Panama. My heart is still full with the joys and struggles of that journey. When I was maybe eight years old, Dad first started planning for the trip. Eighteen years later, we were watching the coast of North Carolina fade away behind us as we set out to sea with three experienced friends, Jane, Rich, and Philippe. How much was I to learn in the next seven days!

The first thing I realized was that, while it was beautifully fresh to keep my cabin's porthole window open on the intercoastal waterway, it was a recipe for soaked bedding at sea. My second lesson followed quickly: although as a child I was never seasick, that had changed – and evidently eating greasy pizza did not improve affairs. I struggled to regain my appetite over the next two days, but was derailed by a storm that blew in. The following three days stretched me greatly. I slept in the dining area, unable to stomach descending to my cabin. Several times a minute, waves would pound the underside of the dining table, making it jump an inch vertically and sounding like a gunshot. The waves became difficult to navigate, and my father took the risk of going outside the cockpit to deploy the storm anchor: a large, underwater parachute that would hold us relatively stationary to ride out the looming swells.

It was there, in the storm, that I struggled to persevere despite my hunger, nausea, and fear. I needed comfort and support. My father was right there. Steadfast Jane kept preparing meals. Yet I couldn't humble myself enough to ask for a simple, needed hug.

Was it pride that kept me from asking for help? Was it fear of relying on another? What a cold, lonely inner landscape I had unexpectedly discovered inside myself. While I timidly swallowed honey, burning my acid seared throat, while I enjoyed a bowl of Jane's delicious stir fry, while, a week later, I slept in a non-rocking bed on the soils of Saint Croix, I quietly chose to become a person who is able to humbly and courageously ask for help.

LEARN TO LOVE

I would ignite that darkened flame inside you
I would bring fire and flame, purging and pain
I would make you truly live
Break you down until you learned to
Love

I would draw you close
I would teach you the mystery of joy
I would teach you to see beauty
To smile, and mean it
I would teach you to
Love

I am jealous over you
I am jealous over you – I made you
I see all you are and all you could be
And I want you to see through my eyes
Love

CHAPTER 10

Companionship

Proverbs 17:17 (ESV)
A friend loves at all times, and a brother is born for adversity.

My first class of my college experience was an evening Western Civilization course. It was in that class that I would meet two girls, Michaela White and Anna Pulscher, who would go on to become my partners in crime for the next year and a half. From playing dress-ups in the pool, to exploring tunnels, to swing dancing, to our parody benevolent mischief done as Those (theta omega zeta epsilon) Girls, we kept ourselves busy. My friend Eric Maggio took Anna and me to a freshman dance, capturing memories that would travel back to Anna's home in South Dakota. Her younger brother Toby would see the photo, and for some reason depart from his usual practice of drawing dragons and stalwart horses to draw my face.

A year later, Toby would travel to visit his sister Anna, who had generously described Toby's soccer skills. I took my skepticism to the soccer field and was soundly rewarded by being nutmegged. He did have skills and speed.

My brother was in the area too – he was finishing his final year of an engineering degree at the same school, and I enjoyed getting to see him from time to time. During our first year of college, Anna had joined my brother and me going out to dinner with my Dad when he came to visit. Anna's and my brother Will's friendship would grow

51

over the years and lead to their engagement in 2000. Christmas of 2000, my entire family visited Anna's family of seven in South Dakota. I watched Toby develop his woodworking and juggling skills, and he initiated a brief, friendly battle for a blanket with me. It was after that more extended meeting that, one evening in the quiet of his room, Toby would offer a brief prayer for a friend like me.

In the next months, I worked up the courage to call Toby under the guise of needing his creative guidance with my wedding gift for our siblings. Toby emailed me for the first time.

During wedding brouhaha, I was able to join Toby's family camping in the Black Hills and experiencing the joy of learning to ride off-road motorcycles. We were in the wedding together, and the night after, during the craziness of a family leg wrestling tournament, Toby did a push up with a clap behind the back. I tried too, and cracked my front tooth.

It was in the Black Hills that Toby and I, both lovers of running, would develop our first tradition: a dawn run up and down a mountain. The beauty those mornings was rich.

One evening by the fire, he asked me about my parents' separation and expressed sorrow for it. To my memory, he was only the second person to ever make the effort to do so, and it meant a lot to me.

The following year, I invited Toby to my senior year February Formal. He came, at the cost of missing tryouts for the Sioux Falls soccer team. I tried to craft a good experience for him, but finding out about the soccer conflict and then me losing my wallet in Chicago (leaving me nearly out of food for the weekend) and Toby's quiet nature conspired to leave me in tears afterward. It felt like a failure. A few weeks later I would receive a package from South Dakota, a handcarved, wooden rose, a small token that he had, in fact, enjoyed himself.

Several months later, I graduated and joined Will, Anna, and Toby on a camping trip to Yosemite. Once again, Toby and I reveled in the joy of early morning runs, with bear cubs and wildflowers. One afternoon while crossing a river, an angry water snake loomed threateningly above the water, and Toby protectively grabbed my hand.

These were the beginnings of love. Little moments of shared joys and sorrow. Companionship in faith, adventure, and artistry. Stubborn, slow determination and tender hearts that would pledge faithfulness in sickness and health seven years later. I have a good friend to go through life with.

TO KEEP A PROMISE

Hand in hand, two lives like vines entwining
Striving together toward the sun
A promise given
And the daily work of a promise kept

This broken world brought home
By the withered branch of wasted muscle
The vines entwined still stand
Thanks to a quiet strength
And a promise kept

The sun still shines
And the rains still fall
And seasons pass
Expectations changing in the tears of rain
New growth forged in the sun
Seasons pass, green turns to brown
Lives slowly spent in gratitude
And the promise kept

CHAPTER 11

Children

3 John 4 (ESV)

I have no greater joy than to hear that my children are walking in the truth.

There are many ways in which I have been spoiled in life. My family wanted me and loved me and taught me. We had a good house and plenty of food. I've had medical and dental care. I've had freedom to choose my beliefs and course in life. I've had a good brain and body for many years. I've had higher education and travel experiences. And, dear to my heart, I have had the gift of mothering children. I know that is not a gift every woman gets, and I am grateful that God allowed me that joy. I didn't get good at childbirth until my third child - it took me that long to recognize that in the absence of fetal distress, no one had the right to dictate how my labor should go except my body. Once I learned to decline unhelpful suggestions and instead follow my body's dictates, birthing became less stressful and less damaging, allowing for a more smooth transition for these little conscious creations of flesh and bone into the great world of light and sound. Malcolm, the performer who loves to connect with people. Oliver, both lover and fighter who feels deeply. Mercedes, loving creatures and loving to both copy and create. These children have opened my eyes to my own selfishness and laziness, teaching me to be a better mother. These children give me immense joy, just getting to witness their daily discoveries, joys, and sorrow. Childhood is a busy but very sweet time of wonder and correction, training little shoots to head toward the light.

I'm thankful for my many gifts, but I am especially thankful for this gift of motherhood.

JOY OF GOLD

It's an early morning day-to-day
Baby's crying, kids quiet at play
I look out across the summer corn
Tall and green from summer sun and summer storm

In the early morning day-to-day
My heart is aching but I don't know how to pray
That simple joy in simple work be born
After weathering hot summer sun and summer storm

I glory in the beauty of a day
The dishes, the diapers, the rhythms beating slow
The simple moments hold
Simple space to grow
This heart from joy of green to joy of gold

It's an early morning day-to-day
Baby's sleeping, kids are still at play
I am growing bit by bit like summer corn
O God may I unfold Autumn's leaf and fruit of gold
After weathering hot summer sun and summer storm

CHAPTER 12

Support

John 13:34–35 (ESV)
A new commandment I give to you, that you love one another: just as I have loved you, you also are to love one another. By this all people will know that you are my disciples, if you have love for one another.

It is worth saying again, I am not enough. I need support, sometimes more than others. A community of fervent prayer has no equal when it comes to support.

It was early September. The corn stood tall and brown, the beautiful stray cat we had adopted was frolicking around the property, and my sixteen-month-old child and I were ready to enjoy the beautiful day. Toby was off at work, and I had two main goals for my day: continue working to scrape off the peeling white paint from our house, and work on learning to smoothly play the processional on guitar for a wedding that weekend. The bright morning was perfect, and my little Malcolm joined in with Penny's joyful explorations. Following her around the trees and branches on the edge of our shelter belt, his fat little hands and bare feet were dusted with dirt. I took a break from scraping, sitting on the steps of our little porch with water bottle and guitar. Little Malcolm came close and reached for my bottle. Not wanting little brown paw prints to adorn my bottle, I held the top close to his mouth without letting him hold it. A grumpy protest noise met my offer, and he whirled and ran toward our gnarled box elder a few feet away. I let him go, returning to another run through on my guitar. I finished the piece, looked up, and was met with still silence.

I put down my guitar, walked out beyond the tree, called ~ nothing. I ran down the edge of our shelter belt, through the trees, around our house ~ nothing. A wave of guilt and shame washed over me. I had one main job as a mother, and I had failed at it.

I knew that the most likely place he had gone was into the cornfield, but I hesitated to enter it lest he should come out while I was in and head toward the road. Numbly, I called my husband and told him. He recommended waiting a little more before calling for help. So I sat. I called my close friend who had given birth ten days before I had, and she recommended calling for help more quickly. When we hung up, she called her church. Christina, the church leaders, and the first police car came. Christina's church family formed a circle and prayed, then started searching. I started answering questions for the first time.

"May we search the house?"

"You are welcome to, but he is not able to open doors so he can't be in there."

My friend Lisa appeared, eyes full of compassion and concern. My eyes misted as I saw reflected to me the heart-wrenching concern that dwelt silently inside me. But I would be no better off if I fell apart and I would be less of a help and more of a liability, so I kept my anguish quiet and inside.

"What does he like? We could talk about that as we call for him in the cornfield."

"He likes balls and airplanes. Thanks."

Toby arrived. I was questioned a second time by a different department, with obvious doubts of my integrity. The yard was completely filled with vehicles, spilling out onto the road.

"We are checking the sloughs."

"You are welcome to, but he wouldn't have gone that way. There are too many prickers and he didn't have shoes on."

Dogs were called in.

I flashed back to twenty years earlier.

It was evening and Dad got a call from Gambrill State Park. The park closed at dusk, and one of our vehicles was parked there. Dad and I drove up and walked some of the trails in the darkness, calling for Mom. We returned home and I was told to gather some of her dirty clothes for the dogs to work from. Around eight the next morning, she had been found, having accidentally taken the one trail that was not a loop trail. I was twelve years old.

Immediately, I gathered a bundle of Malcolm's dirty clothes. The dogs came, but they were kept on the leash and didn't seem to be able to find a good trail.

"Do you have any wells or cisterns?"

I was pulled aside into a police car for over an hour of detailed questioning. This officer was more compassionate, but it was still obvious he was searching for a possible motive for foul play.

He finally finished his questioning, and I excused myself to the restroom. It was my first break since the nightmare began.

Someone knocked on the door. I ignored them. I was tired, but I finished and opened the door. I was immediately greeted by an officer who told me Malcolm had been found. I walked out by the cornfield and waited for my beloved child. Slowly he was carried to my arms. He was calm and curious about the emergency vehicles. A large smudge of dirt covered one side of his face, evidence of a nap.

A tear streak split the smudge. He had cried.

It had been four long hours, and I knew he must be hungry and thirsty, so I took him inside and nursed him. Many vehicles were leaving when we came back out, and the gentleman from Christina's church who had found my child left quietly, without recognition.

That night, I wandered the house, unable to sleep.

Sometimes, I make serious mistakes that I can't fix. Sometimes my integrity will be doubted. And sometimes, the body of Christ will stand with me in faith and precious action in the middle of my mess.

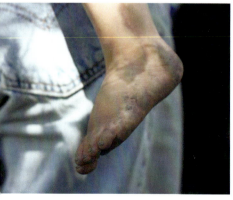

LITTLE LOST CHILD

I am your comfort
Walk in my rest
Lay this your burden here against my chest
I am your helper
I see your need
I hear your heart's cry and I help you believe
I am here
I am God
I am ever always with you

I am his comfort
He walks in my rest
I hold his small form close to my chest
I am his helper
I do not leave
I hear his heart's cry and I help him believe
I am here
I am God
I am ever always with you

Sometimes you may lose what you hold most precious
Sometimes what you fear may come to be
My child when the whelming flood surrounds you
A firm foundation you have in me

I am here

I am God

I am ever always with you

On Christ the solid rock I stand

All other ground is sinking sand

CHAPTER 13

Spirit, Come

Ephesians 2:10 (ESV)
For we are his workmanship, created in Christ Jesus for good works,
which God prepared beforehand, that we should walk in them.

The big, South Dakota sky, the silence broken by bird song, the staid trees, and the gentle breath of a breeze. From the vantage point of a small, weathered porch containing cat and child, I carried on my conversation with the source of the quiet beauty around me. My heart was yearning for more. For confidence in and expectation of and reliance on the elusive third person of the trinity. More! Not just for myself, but for the community of believers at large. Lord, use me.

The morning passed into the everyday duties of the home, but my heart cry was heard in heaven, and my life would be changed.

When I think of being used by God, I have images of conversations, pastors, missionaries. My first association is not the slow progression of sickness. As is often the case, I asked for something, not realizing the possible implications of God's choice to fulfill my request (yes, I have also prayed for patience before, something I am not sure that I would ever recommend doing).

God chose to use me in his work of spreading his Spirit more fully in his church by allowing me to suddenly crumple while I attempted a handstand. By allowing my fingers to not obey me when, hungry and chilled, I tried to zip up my children's jackets. By allowing me to lose my grip on my guitar pick while playing. I gave birth to my third beautiful child, and afterward I could no longer straighten my fingers. I knew something was not right, but I was not sure what it was. Lying in bed one evening, God gently whispered ALS to me. I could remember ice bucket challenge "fail" videos, but I could not remember what the disease entailed, so I looked it up and noted that it was a possibility.

A month went by. I visited a chiropractor and a neurologist for the first time ever. I discovered the EMG torture device and diagnostic tool, I had my first MRI.

One evening in the silence of our empty church, I stood with tears in my eyes and told God I didn't want to do this. I didn't want to slowly transition to a wheelchair, unable to eat, talk, or breathe. But he was quiet.

It is going to happen, and it is going to be okay. I'm in control and I never go back on my word. You love me and I called you to myself according to my purposes, and therefore all things I allow in your life ~ including ALS ~ are working together for good.

We didn't cry when we got the diagnosis confirmation. I already knew what the assessment would be from the test results. I knew that, if I truly believed my loving God was in control, I would trust him. There were still moments of hot tears. But even in the middle of my mess, God was busy making his new genesis, as he is wont to do.

God was in control then, and he has still quietly displayed his control through the dreaded progression. Five years into the disease, I was bound to a wheelchair, ate through a feeding tube, was becoming difficult to understand, and relied on 24-7 noninvasive ventilation to breathe. Slowly, I became unable to sleep as each time I would doze off, I would inhale my saliva. The human body can only handle so much sleep deprivation. I eventually felt that I needed to go to the emergency room to ask for a trach, as recommended previously by my pulmonologist should we feel it necessary after hours. Every so often, a wave of fatigue would wash over me. I would ask Toby to rub my back, and I would feel stronger again. Slowly, the waves came more often and the rubbing held less and less power. I knew something was going to happen that I could not control. I felt God's peace that whatever happened was going to be okay. I wanted Toby to know the same assurance, so I typed with my eyes "Something is going to happen and it is going to be okay." Shortly after, my husband had to witness the harrowing ordeal of watching his wife lose consciousness, stop breathing, and be intubated. God's gentle hand was with us again.

There is yet another story of God's miraculous provision for Toby and me in this disease, but it is a story just for the two of us.

I don't know exactly what God is doing with letting me develop ALS, but I do know that he is in control of all parts of this disease, and I know that he loves me. He knows more than I do, and I trust him. And while I have struggled as that trust has grown, he has even given me these little, miraculous manifestations of his Spirit. God is faithfully using me, as I offered.

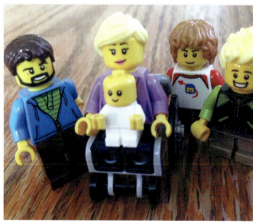

SARA

Sara, I have looked up to you
You have given my heart a voice
You have given my pain a song
You, who bring the great Silence a little closer
Singer of songs
You are revelation

These years keep slipping along
I somehow thought I'd have come further by now
But I'm right back where I began
Cold heart, searching for truth
Trying to hold together the pieces

But I don't have it together
And I don't have much to give
I, I made a mess
Can You clean it up?

And I, I look up to You
You have given my heart a voice
You have given my pain a song
O great Silence speak
O great Singer of Songs
Make me revelation!

CHAPTER 14

God, Sickness, and Healing

Daniel 3:16–18 (ESV)
Shadrach, Meshach, and Abednego answered and said to the king, "O
Nebuchadnezzar, we have no need to answer you in this matter. If this
be so, our God whom we serve is able to deliver us from the burning
fiery furnace, and he will deliver us out of your hand, O king. But if
not, be it known to you, O king, that we will not serve your gods or
worship the golden image that you have set up."

No one wants their friend to go through the difficulty of an ALS diagnosis. Once one gets diagnosed, loved ones and friends and acquaintances start offering ideas for and pathways to healing. Some suggestions are physical. I've tried some pretty unusual therapies, from infrared light to getting stung by bees to fecal transplant. Other suggestions are spiritual. I've watched Curry Blake, Andrew Murray, Sam Storms, Marilyn Hickey, Andrew Wommack, and Jackie Pullinger, and I have listened to George Muller's writings. There are many different approaches to miracles.

As I processed my parents' marriage difficulties and the pain it caused me, I came to some firm conclusions about the supernatural: my heart should hope for good even when it seems impossible; in the middle of the pain, God is still present, powerful, and good. It took me about twenty years to shape my beliefs from that experience – I am a slow processor! But that struggle would help guide me through the difficulties to come.

ALS. It's easy to ask for healing from a head cold. It is easy to shy away from asking for complete healing when the obstacle looms large, like stage four cancer, depression, addiction, and ALS. We don't often see miraculous healing from the big things. But let us be sure that the reason is not because we have neglected to ask for the healing. God is powerful enough to do it. Jesus promised we would do even bigger miracles than he performed. And the history of the church is littered with testimony to continued healings and miracles. We can pray for miraculous healing from big things with confidence.

Here in the slow decay of ALS, I have had a lot of time to think about my theology of healing. My reading of the Bible and listening to different people's thoughts have led to the following beliefs.

God knows all my days before they happen. God allows bad things to happen to people whom he loves (including disease), but he promises that they will work to accomplish good. Physical healing from sickness is provided in the atonement, but timing is variable (now or after death are both possibilities). We are told to ask and we will receive, we are told to persevere in asking, and we are encouraged to have faith. We are told that some actions can hinder prayers. It is expected that we will all die once, as Christians we are promised an Advocate during judgment after death, and we are promised eternal life with God close to us. I think it is important to remember that we are looking forward to a better home, a new Earth, and a body version 2.0. Death is difficult, but the keys of death and hell are in the hands of our loving Advocate. We are destined for life beyond the grave, whether or not we experience miraculous healing before death.

I do not believe that I am guaranteed physical healing in this life, even if I have enough faith and take dominion over ALS. I think it is also good to remember that not once did Jesus rebuke a sick person for lack of faith (although he did commend its presence). He repeatedly showed compassion toward the sick and took time to heal them. Today, it is not uncommon to find teachers of healing who are quite willing to regale with stories of their past healings but fail to follow in Jesus' footsteps in these areas.

I believe that the Spirit loves to give gifts of healing at his discretion. God is in control, and God is compassionate, and he loves to give good gifts to his children.

This is what I have come to believe, and this is my firm hope.

So I believe God knew I would get ALS, he will use it for good, he will heal me, and I will keep asking for healing in this life until he either heals me or takes me to be with him.

It is not easy to continue with faith for years when you don't see the miracle. The passage of years, though, does not mean the miracle won't happen. Nearly twenty-five years after their separation, God answered my prayers for my separated parents with a yes: my treasured parents got back together. With God's help, I will persevere similarly in my prayers for healing from this mysterious, incurable disease.

THE GOD WHO HEALS

I will meditate on your promises, faithful God
Strong in power and might
And tender enough to watch over
This sparrow

You whose eyes roam to and fro over the whole earth
To give strong support to those
Whose hearts are blameless
Toward you

There is none like God, O Jeshurun
Riding through the heavens to your help
Underneath me are your
Everlasting arms

Heal me and I shall be healed
Forgive all my many faults
Heal all my diseases
Yahweh Rapha, the God who heals

Oh I know the eternal God is my dwelling place
And I am a citizen of a far country
And what is mortal must be swallowed up in life
Yet still you are mindful of me
This little fading flower of the field
You, who were moved to tears by our grief
You are mindful of me

So here in my distress I cry out to you
The only one with power to save
You can, you will, and even if you don't
I will worship you

Heal me and I shall be healed
Forgive all my many faults
Heal all my diseases
Yahweh Rapha, the God who heals

CHAPTER 15

Guided

Psalm 139:23–24 (ESV)
Search me, O God, and know my heart! Try me and know my thoughts! And
see if there be any grievous way in me, and lead me in the way everlasting!

I had the deep pleasure of working coordinating music for our church, River Community Church, from 2012 until 2016. In late 2015, I could no longer use my fingers to play guitar due to muscle weakness from ALS. Music and art and poetry have filled me with joy since I was young. It felt wonderful to be paid to do something I loved so much, and to know that my service and skills were valued, and for the culmination of my efforts to aid myself and others in something that was so dear to my heart ~ worshiping the God of the Bible. I've had much time to think about my contribution in these years of growing stillness and silence. I can see how my insecurities made it difficult for gentleness and space to enter the music, leaving me to rely too heavily on constant instrumentation. I can see how my disorganization hampered all of us from growing. And most seriously, I can see how I enjoyed the spotlight. I wanted to glorify God, but my sick soul didn't mind if I got a little glory too in the process.

Even my best efforts are tainted. I want to be pure. I'm confident that God has taught and will continue to teach me to be pure. ALS gives me no free pass ~ I am infinitely creative at finding ways to inadequately complete my duties even now. How easy it is to slip into the drug-like oblivion of self-entertainment rather than engaging directly with the people around me.

I am a collection of missteps and clouded motives, yet my guide leads me toward truth with gentleness and honor. He knows my guilt, but covers it up at his own expense. He looks at me with love, knowing that his sometimes painful correction will create good in me. You can't compete with that love ~ not even my treasured husband, children, brother, and parents. Other people speak into my life, and I often glean helpful nuggets from them. Other people sometimes go beyond and seek to master my path. But I am bound with the sweet uncomparable ties of gentleness and honor. Only one masters me.

I am grateful to have a patient, wise, and loving guide to lead me through the trickery of my own heart.

YOU ARE WITH ME

You lead the blind
In a way that they do not know
I don't know where I'm going
But I know you are here

In paths that they
Do not know You will guide
I can't see the pathway
You still see clear

You are with me
You do not forsake Your child

You turn the darkness before me to light
The rough places to level ground
These are the things that you do
You walk with Your child through the night

You are with me
You do not forsake Your child

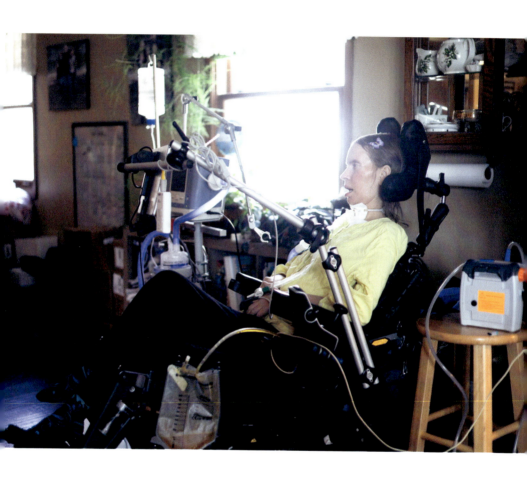

CHAPTER 16

Perseverance

1 Peter 4:19 (ESV)
Therefore let those who suffer according to God's will entrust their souls
to a faithful Creator while doing good.

Looking back upon this string of stories, one might be tempted to think that my life is littered with negative experiences. While I have faced and do face challenges, they have hardly characterized the bulk of my experiences. My challenges have, however, played key roles in forming my faith, and since it has been my goal to describe that invisible journey, I have been happy to share them with you. Before I leave you, I feel I must share one final glimpse into the forging of my faith.

How difficult it is to persevere! My current job is to persevere through disease. I am surrounded by friends quietly doing the same: cancer, fibromyalgia, heart defects, tumors. There are others persevering through seasonal depression, anxiety, being bipolar. Some are persevering in love and boundaries through painful personality disorders in people close to them. I believe that all of us, at one time or another, find ourselves needing to persevere. We are not alone.

My particular brand of perseverance is not unique. I have the honor of walking with friends in South Dakota and even, through Facebook and YouTube, around the world who have fought to thrive despite the disease of ALS. Mothers, fathers, husbands, wives, single people, older individuals, even children (yes, people under eighteen get this disease). Much of what I struggle with, these souls also know from experience.

My belief is that God has work for me to do, no matter what my situation is, and that my job is to do that work while I am able. He can be the one in charge of why he let me have this disease, and he can explain it to me and comfort me later like Lazarus in Abraham's arms. He can decide the timing of my healing, although I ask for healing this side of heaven.

So, what is a quadriplegic, nonverbal woman with a trach and feeding tube still good for? What value is there in such an expensive, restricted, unglamorous life that puts such a weight on caregivers?

I have many limitations. It is embarrassing to drool with my mouth hanging open. It is unpleasant to have someone else brush my teeth in a way that is different from how I would have. I would prefer not to need other people to help me use the facilities. I miss the pleasure of eating and swallowing. I miss running and hugging and cuddling. I miss my voice.

And yet, despite these limitations, there are things I can do. I can show love to my husband and children, exploring their thoughts and experiences. I can encourage my husband. I can make his life a little easier by scheduling our caregivers and life events, and by scheduling meals. I can invest in the kids, helping to encourage kindness and trying to guide them into beneficial life habits (challenging task!). I can be involved in encouraging friends far and wide through Facebook. I can help other people with the ALS diagnosis have a better idea what to expect through a YouTube video blog. I can enjoy the antics of my kids, the sounds of summer storms, the fresh, cool breezes of autumn, the bite of winter's cold, the gentle massage of a friend, losing at Scrabble, learning online. I can worship God with my friends. I can feed myself from the Bible. I can talk with God. And I can share my life with you in hopes that something in my journey will help you in yours.

But even though I can do all these things, it often takes work to actually do them. There are some days where I am only hampered by my own laziness. Other days, however, I am forced to just grab on to God and hold on. Those days, I face my utter need for his strength. The day I could no longer have my baby girl with me throughout the day, giving her away for daily care into the arms of a loving friend. The several times I had difficulty breathing when no one was near to help. Dealing with pain in the hospital and not knowing when I would be able to leave. Feeling the effects of tachycardia above 120 beats per minute for hours on end after being in the same room as something I am allergic to. Days like these I feel how much I need God every hour, I am driven to him. I reach the end of myself and just hold on to him. I rely on a God who promises to be with me, in life, through death, and into life part two.

Perseverance is possible. And through my priceless, slow struggle to do the work God has for me, I learn obedience. I trust him. It will be okay.

WE WHO SUFFER

Oh Abram you did not see you could not know
The future but God spoke and you did go
Oh Sarai there were many days, empty years
Waiting to exchange laughter for your tears

I am Hannah giving up my little Samuel
I'm in Ruth's unknown land not as we'd planned
Walking not by sight but by faith
My future is yours to mold
You may break but you will hold

One Lazarus died and lived again
One did not
Both believed and they both were faithful men
I see Paul a drink offering, the Baptist wondering
I see my own Jesus faithfully suffering

I believe you are strong I believe you care
I believe in the suffering you are there
You tell me to keep asking and not despair
Silence greets my mustard seed
You help me lose all and still believe

Let those who suffer
We who suffer
According to God's will

Continue entrusting

Ourselves to our oh so faithful Creator

While we do good

EPILOGUE

My story is not done: I'm still breathing (thanks to technology). There is no tidy bow to conclude my story. I love closure, but my earthside story is still daily developing. All the same, I must finish this book somewhere, so this little collection of stories is my completed gift to you.

Now go share your story.

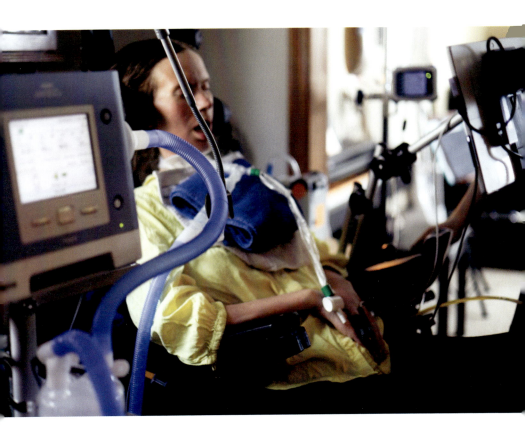

THE PARADE

In a Constant parade from birth to the grave
O soul grow strong and stand
Add your voice into the throng
God laid this time in your hand

Rise up, set your bearing true
Then sing the crowd your song
Trample fear and the bitter bonds
Keeping your voice from rising strong

Let pain and beauty strip your heart raw
May you soft and tender be
So to echo forth to man and God
True reflections of love you see

True reflections, few reflections – precious, precious few
Precious drops that join the flow
Of passioned, pained praises that rise like incense
And salve in ways you'll never know

Not one drop not one single drop
Is forgotten, held soft by the hand
That first gave all and will give again
Once you've taken your brief stand

So look left, look right, your part will soon end
Soul stand and do your best
To grave from birth and shadowed beyond
We stand and then we rest

ACKNOWLEDGMENTS

This creation has been a team effort lovingly watched over by God. This book could not have come together without the careful eye of my editor and friend, Sheri Levisay. Amie Delgado, your artistic eye has blessed my book with the beauty of your photos. Jen Pfeiffer, your layout work and patience with my unending revisions is legendary. You have done beautiful work. I offer my gratitude for the sincere input of Dr. Tom Hanks. Dad, thank you for being my constant cheerleader. The spiritual, emotional, physical, and financial support of our friends at River Community Church and our small town of Dell Rapids has buoyed our family, giving me the opportunity to spend more time on pursuits like this book. Truly, the support has reached far beyond our little town. And all this could never have happened without the faithful work of caregivers who lovingly tend to the mundane needs of my daily life: Johanna Wollman, Sam Mertz, Sandy Koenig, Ronda Golden, my dear mom, and, most of all, my rock of a husband. Toby, you've laid down your preferences and life for me. This book is only one of many things that your commitment has made possible.